Fools

A COMIC FABLE

by Neil Simon 1927-

SAMUEL FRENCH, INC.

25 WEST 45TH STREET   NEW YORK 10036
7623 SUNSET BOULEVARD   HOLLYWOOD 90046
LONDON   *TORONTO*

Please be advised that Samuel French, Inc. can supply amateurs a music tape of the original Broadway Production *upon receipt* of the following:

1. $25.00 Special Deposit. This deposit is refunded when the tape is returned.
2. $10.00 non-refundable Rental Fee.
3. A music royalty of $10.00 for each performance planned.
4. $2.50 First Class Mailing and Handling Charge.
5. Exact performance dates.

Please note that the tape is loaned for a period of 8 weeks only.

Please allow one week for delivery.

Stock royalty terms quoted upon application.

FOR BABA

FOOLS was first presented by Emanuel Azenberg on April 6, 1981, at the Eugene O'Neill Theatre, New York City, with the following cast:

(In order of appearance)

LEON TOLCHINSKY	*John Rubinstein*
SNETSKY	*Gerald Hiken*
MAGISTRATE	*Fred Stuthman*
SLOVITCH	*David Lipman*
MISHKIN	*Joseph Leon*
YENCHNA	*Florence Stanley*
DR. ZUBRITSKY	*Harold Gould*
LENYA ZUBRITSKY	*Mary Louise Wilson*
SOPHIA ZUBRITSKY	*Pamela Reed*
GREGOR YOUSEKEVITCH	*Richard B. Shull*

Directed by Mike Nichols

Scenery by John Lee Beatty

Costumes by Patricia Zipprodt

Lighting by Tharon Musser

THE SETTING

TIME: Long ago

PLACE: The village of Kulyenchikov

Act One

Fools

Scene 1

*Kulyenchikov, about 1890, a remote Ukrainian
village. Leon Tolchinsky, about thirty, carrying a
battered old suitcase and some books tied together,
arrives over a small bridge in the town square. He
looks around, seems pleased, then turns to the audience.*

Leon. (*Smiles.*) Kulyenchikov, I like it! It's exactly as
I pictured: a quiet, pleasant village, not too large . . . the
perfect place for a new schoolteacher to begin his career
. . . Well, to be honest, I did spend mornings for two
years in a small children's school in Moscow teaching
tiny tots rudimentary spelling and numbers, but this,
this is my first bona-fide, professional appointment as a
full-time schoolmaster. Acutally, I never even heard of
Kulyenchikov until I saw the advertisement that a Dr.
Zubritsky placed in the college journal. Although the
position was in a remote village in the Ukraine, I
jumped at the chance, but I don't mind telling you that
my heart is pounding with excitement. I have this passion for teaching . . . Greek, Latin, astronomy, classic
literature. I get goose bumps just thinking about it . . .
(*He looks around.*) I don't see anyone around . . .
Maybe I arrived a little early — I'm one of those extremely eager and enthusiastic people who's up at the crack of
dawn, ready to begin his work. This is a very, very
auspicious day in my life. (*We hear a ram's horn offstage.*) Oh! Excuse me.

9

(SNETSKY *the shepherd enters, carrying a ram's horn and a staff.*)

SNETSKY. Elenya! Lebidoff! Marushka! Olga! Where are you?

LEON. Good morning.

SNETSKY. Good morning. Did you happen to see two dozen sheep?

LEON. Two dozen sheep?

SNETSKY. Yes. There were fourteen of them. (*He continues looking.*)

LEON. No. I'm sorry.

SNETSKY. Well, if you see them, would you give them a message?

LEON. A message for the sheep?

SNETSKY. Yes, tell them the shepherd is looking for them and they should tell you where they are and I'll come and get them. Thank you. (*He starts to walk off.*)

LEON. Wait, wait. Excuse me—what is your name, please?

SNETSKY. (*Stops.*) Snetsky.

LEON. And your first name?

SNETSKY. (*Thinks.*) How soon do you need it?

LEON. Never mind. Forget your first name.

SNETSKY. I did.

LEON. I am Leon Steponovitch Tolchinsky and I am to be the new schoolteacher.

SNETSKY. Is that a fact? (*He shakes* LEON's *hand vigorously.*) I'm very honored to meet you, Leon Steponovitch Tolchinsky. I am Something Something Snetsky . . . Will you be staying the night?

LEON. You don't understand. Kulyenchikov will be my new home. I'm going to live here and teach here. I am, if I may say so, an excellent teacher.

SNETSKY. Oh, they all were. They came by the thousands, but not one of them lasted through the first night. (*He blows the horn hard.*) Oh, it's so hard to blow these, I don't know how the sheep do it.

LEON. You've had thousands of teachers?

SNETSKY. More. Hundreds! We're unteachable. We're all stupid in Kulyenchikov. There isn't a town or village more stupid in all of Mother Poland.

LEON. Russia.

SNETSKY. Whatever. All good people, mind you, but not a decent brain among them. (*He blows the horn with difficulty.*) Oh, that feels so good. I just opened up my ears. I thought you were whispering. What were you saying?

LEON. Are you telling me that every man, woman and child—

SNETSKY. All stupid. Including me. Talk to me another ten minutes and you'll begin to notice.

LEON. (*Ignores it.*) I was hired by Dr. Zubritsky to teach his young daughter.

SNETSKY. (*Bursts out laughing.*) Teach his daughter? Impossible. The girl is hopeless. Nineteen years old and she just recently learned to sit down . . . She's hopeless. She doesn't even know the difference between a cow and a duck. Not that it's an easy subject, mind you.

LEON. (*To the audience.*) Something is up here! (*He takes the ad out of his pocket.*) I thought nothing of it then, but when I first read it I *did* notice that every word in the advertisement was misspelled . . . I'm sure Dr. Zubritsky will explain it all to me. (*He steps back and turns to* SNETSKY.) You've been most helpful, Citizen Snetsky. I enjoyed our chat.

SNETSKY. As did I, Master Tolchinsky. (*He turns to*

the audience.) He's not the only one who can have private thoughts. I can have private thoughts as well. (*He tries to think.*) The trouble is, I can never think of a thought to have in private. Oh, I must be on my way. Good day, schoolmaster.

LEON. I'm sure we'll meet again.

SNETSKY. Oh, of course. Just mention my name to anyone. Snetsky the sheep loser. (*He leaves. A* MAGISTRATE, *ringing a bell, enters.* LEON *tries to stop him, but is ignored.*)

MAGISTRATE. Nine o'clock and all's well . . . Nine o'clock in the village of Kulyenchikov and all's well . . . Nine o'clock and all's well. (*He is gone.*)

LEON. (*To the audience.*) It may have been all well with him, but I was beginning to have my doubts. (*He leaves. A butcher,* SLOVITCH, *comes out of his shop with a broom. He sweeps the dirt into a pile and then sweeps it* into *the shop. The postman,* MISHKIN, *appears.*)

SCENE 2

SLOVITCH. Good morning, postman.

MISHKIN. Good morning, butcher.

SLOVITCH. A beautiful, sunny day, isn't it?

MISHKIN. Is it? I haven't looked up yet. (*He looks up.*) Oh, yes. Lovely. Very nice.

SLOVITCH. Do I have any mail?

MISHKIN. No. I'm sorry. I'm the postman. I have all the mail.

SLOVITCH. My sister in Odessa hasn't been feeling well. I was hoping I would hear from her.

MISHKIN. It's very hard to hear all the way from Odessa. Perhaps she wrote a letter. I'll look. (*He starts to look through the mail. We hear* YENCHNA, *a vendor, calling "Fish!" offstage before she appears.*)

YENCHNA. (*Calling out, selling her wares.*) Fish! Fresh fish! Nice fresh flounder and halibut! A good piece of carp for lunch. (*She has no fish, but bunches of flowers.*)

SLOVITCH. Good morning, Yenchna.

YENCHNA. How about a nice piece of haddock? Is that a beautiful fish?

SLOVITCH. What do you mean fish? Those are flowers.

YENCHNA. They didn't catch anything today. Why should I suffer because the fisherman had a bad day? Try the carp, it smells gorgeous.

MISHKIN. I don't have any letters from your sister, Slovitch. But I have a nice letter from the shoemaker's cousin. Would you like that?

SLOVITCH. Is she sick? I hate reading bad news.

MISHKIN. No, no. In perfect health. Take it. You'll enjoy it.

YENCHNA. Can you believe my daughter hasn't written to me in over a year?

MISHKIN. Doesn't your daughter live with you?

YENCHNA. It's a good thing. Otherwise I'd never hear from her. (LEON *enters.*)

LEON. (*To the townspeople.*) Good morning. My name is Leon Steponovitch Tolchinsky. I'm the new schoolmaster.

MISHKIN. (*Bows.*) Mishkin the postman.

SLOVITCH. (*Bows.*) Slovitch the butcher.

YENCHNA. Yenchna the vendor.

LEON. How do you do. I was just talking to a shepherd named Snetsky.

MISHKIN. Oh, yes. Something Something Snetsky. We know him well.

LEON. He was pleasant enough, although—and I hope I don't seem unkind—somewhat deficient in his mental alertness.

YENCHNA. That's Snetsky, all right. (*She taps her head.*) He was kicked in the head by a horse.

LEON. Oh, well. What a pity. When was that?

YENCHNA. Tuesday, Wednesday, twice on Friday and all day Saturday.

LEON. (*Looks at* YENCHNA's *flowers.*) What lovely and fragrant wares you have to sell, madame. Perhaps I might buy some for my new employer. How much are they, please?

YENCHNA. The flounder is two kopecks and the halibut is three.

LEON. I beg your pardon?

YENCHNA. (*Holds up a white flower.*) If it's too much, I have a nice whitefish for one and a half. (*She wraps it in a newspaper and hands it to him. He pays.*)

LEON. (*To the audience.*) Perhaps the dialect is a little different in this part of the country. (*To the group.*) I'm very eager to begin my new duties. Will one of you be so kind as to direct me to the home of Dr. Zubrisky? (*They all point in different directions.*)

ALL THREE. That way!

LEON. Thank you. Perhaps I'll go in the one direction you haven't pointed to . . . A pleasure meeting you all. (SNETSKY *appears.*) Oh, Hello again. Have you found your sheep?

SNETSKY. Not yet. (LEON *leaves.*) Who was that?

MISHKIN. The new schoolteacher.

SNETSKY. Another one? I just met one a few minutes ago, they must be having a convention here.

YENCHNA. Count Yousekevitch up on the hill isn't going to be very happy about this.

SLOVITCH. That's right. Count Yousekevitch doesn't like new schoolteachers.

SNETSKY. Why?

MISHKIN. He's afraid they'll break the curse.

SNETSKY. What curse?

SLOVITCH. The one that made us stupid since the day we were born.

SNETSKY. Oh, that one.

MISHKIN. Yes. I've been stupid for fifty-one years . . . What about you, Snetsky?

SNETSKY. I'll be dumb forty-three next July.

MISHKIN. And you, Slovitch?

SLOVITCH. Forty-one for me. What about you, Yenchna?

YENCHNA. I just turned the corner of twenty-six.

SLOVITCH. That corner must be about forty miles from here. (*They all exit.*)

SCENE 3

The home of DR. ZUBRITSKY. *The* DOCTOR *is examining a patient,* MAGISTRATE KUPCHIK. *The* DOCTOR *is administering an eye-chart test.*

MAGISTRATE. (*Covering one eye.*) K . . . E . . . 5 . . . L . . . A . . . R . . . V . . . Is that right?

DOCTOR. I don't know. It sounds good to me. (*Listening to the* MAGISTRATE's *heart.*) Yes . . . Yes . . . Very interesting.

MAGISTRATE. Then I'm in good health?

DOCTOR. The best. The best of health. You'll live to be eighty.

MAGISTRATE. I'm seventy-nine now.

DOCTOR. Well, you've got a wonderful year ahead of you.

MAGISTRATE. (*Gets dressed.*) Good. I must keep up my strength. I'm a magistrate. Law and order must be preserved.

DOCTOR. Did you want a prescription?

MAGISTRATE. For what?

DOCTOR. I don't know. Some people like prescriptions. Here, take this to the druggist. Pick out something you like and take it three times a day with a little water. Goodbye, sir.

MAGISTRATE. How much do I owe you, Doctor?

DOCTOR. Oh, forget it. Forget it. If I ever go to medical school you can send me a little something.

MAGISTRATE. Oh, thank you. Goodbye.

(LENYA *enters. She is exuberant and excited.*)

LENYA. Nikolai! Nikolai! He's here. He's come! He arrived not two minutes ago. He's young. He looks strong, determined. Maybe he'll be the one, Nikolai. Maybe this one will finally be our salvation.

DOCTOR. Calm yourself, Lenya. Who's come? Who'll be our salvation?

LENYA. The new—er—The new—what do you call them? They come and they—er—The ones who—We had one once but no more.

DOCTOR. Oh, God. I know. I know who you mean.

LENYA. They have a place, and then you go to the place—

DOCTOR. And they point to you and they say—er—they ask you if you—er—

LENYA. And if you don't, they say, "Why didn't you? Next time I'll *make* you."

DOCTOR. And he's outside?

LENYA. He's just down the street.

DOCTOR. Well, show him in, Lenya. Show him in. And pray God this is the one who will deliver us and all of Kulyenchikov from this dreadful — er — this — er — Oh, God, what is it we have again?

LENYA. I know. I know what you mean. It sounds like *nurse* . . .

DOCTOR. Nurse.

LENYA. Or *hearse* . . .

DOCTOR. Hearse.

LENYA. Something like that.

DOCTOR. Or something like that. (*There is a knock.*) Or is it a knock?

LENYA. We have a knock? (*She goes to the door.*)

DOCTOR. Yes, yes. Open the knock. (*She pushes on the door.*) The other way, the other way. (*She opens it. LEON stands there.*)

LENYA. Won't you come in, young man?

LEON. Dr. Zubritsky? Madame Zubritsky? I am delighted to be in Kulyenchikov. I am Leon Steponovitch Tolchinsky.

DOCTOR. So you are the new — the new —

LEON. Yes! I am he.

DOCTOR. It's he, Lenya, the new — the new —

LENYA. But you look so young to be a — to be a —

LEON. Not at all. I think in time you will find that I am, if I may say so, one of the best young — well, I don't want to seem immodest.

DOCTOR. No. Please. Be immodest. We *love* immodesty.

LENYA. The more immodest the better. The best young what? *What?*

LEON. The best young teacher in all of Russia!

DOCTOR. (*Excited.*) *A teacher!!!* He's a teacher!! The new teacher is here.

LENYA. *Thank God the teacher is here!!*

LEON. Thank you. Thank you. I'm most gratified at this most warm and overwhelming reception.

DOCTOR. Make yourself at home, teacher. Take off your coat, teacher. Lenya, bring the teacher a cup of tea. Sit down, teacher.

LENYA. Would you like some tea, teacher? Or maybe some paper and pens, teacher? Perhaps you would like to start teaching right away, teacher?

LEON. Well, no one's more eager than I am. ~~Madame~~ Zubritsky, this is for you. (*He hands her the flowers.*)

LENYA. Oh, whitefish. I saw them on sale today. Thank you. (*She takes them.* LEON *looks at the audience, bewildered.*)

DOCTOR. How can we help you?

LEON. Well, there are a few questions I wanted to ask you first.

DOCTOR. Questions! That's what they ask. When they point to you and you don't know. He knows. He knows what questions are. I can tell this one's going to be a good teacher.

LENYA. Would you be so kind, Master Tolchinsky, to—to ask us a question. Any question at all.

DOCTOR. It means a lot to us. It's been so long since anyone has asked us a good "school" question . . . *Please*! (*They all sit.*)

LEON. Well, there are questions and there are question. Do you want a question on mathematics or a question dealing with science or perhaps a philosophical question?

DOCTOR. The first one. The first one sounds good. The philosophical question. Ask us that one.

LEON. Very well, if you wish . . . What is the purpose of man's existence?

DOCTOR. What a question . . . Lenya, did you ever hear such a beautiful question?

LENYA. I'm speechless . . . To think someone would ask *us* a question like that.

LEON. Are you interested in the answer?

DOCTOR. Not today, thank you. To be asked one question like that in a lifetime is more than we ever expected. The answer should be given to someone much more worthy than we are.

LEON. But it's your birthright. Knowledge is *everyone's* birthright.

DOCTOR. Everyone not born in Kulyenchikov.

LEON. I don't understand.

LENYA. You would if you knew about the nurse.

LEON. What nurse?

DOCTOR. Not the nurse, the hearse.

LEON. The hearse?

LENYA. He means the purse.

LEON. What kind of purse?

DOCTOR. The kind of purse that inflicts the wrath of God upon all those poor souls who were unfortunate enough to be born in this pitiful village.

LEON. Do you mean, perhaps, a curse?

DOCTOR. *Curse!!* That's what it is! I *knew* it sounded like that.

LENYA. We were so close. *So* close!

LEON. What is this curse you speak of, Dr. Zubritsky?

DOCTOR. Lenya, bolt the door. Draw the curtains.

LENYA. I can't draw curtains. I can draw a cat or a fish—

DOCTOR. Never mind. Lower your voice.

LENYA. (*Bends her knees, making herself shorter.*) How low do you want my voice?

DOCTOR. That's low enough. Bring the book, it's on the shelf. (*She goes over to the bookshelf, knees bent as she walks. To* LEON.) Young man — have you ever heard of the Curse of Kulyenchikov?

LEON. I can't say that I have.

DOCTOR. You can't say that? It's not hard. Even Lenya can say that.

LENYA. (*Standing by the bookshelf.*) "The Curse of Kulyenchikov."

LEON. What is this curse, Doctor?

DOCTOR. Two hundred years ago, a curse was put on this village that struck down every man, woman, child and domestic animal, including all their ancestors for generations to come, leaving each and every one of them — and this you'll find hard to believe — with no more intelligence than a bump on a log.

LEON. Doctor, I don't believe in curses. Curses are old wives' tales.

DOCTOR. You're thinking of Noychka. In Noychka all the old wives have tails. That was *their* curse. Ours is altogether different.

LEON. But where did the curse come from? And who would inflict such curel punishment on such a peaceful and simple village?

(LENYA *has returned with the book.*)

DOCTOR. Who indeed? It's all documented in *The Book of Curses.* (*He blows dust off the cover into* LEON's *face. To* LENYA.) I thought you said you dusted this.

LENYA. I did. I put dust on it yesterday.

DOCTOR. (*To* LEON.) Here. Read it for yourself. The page is marked.

LEON. (*Opens the book. The page is sticky and gummy.*) It's all stuck together.

LENYA. We marked it with maple syrup. Read it to us. (*They all sit on the* DOCTOR'*s sofa.*)

LEON. (*Reading.*) "On the morning of April II, in the year 1691, in the village of Kulyenchikov, two young people fell hopelessly in love."

LENYA. I knew it. Whenever young people fall in love, you know a curse is coming.

LEON. But surely you've heard all this before?

DOCTOR. Many times. But we never understand it. It's a very well thought out curse.

LENYA. So what happens?

LEON. "The boy was a young, handsome but illiterate farmer named Casimir Yousekevitch. The girl was the daughter of the most learned man in the town, Mikhail Zubritsky."

LENYA. Zubritsky! I've heard that name before.

DOCTOR. I've seen it! I've seen it! On a front door somewhere. In this neighborhood.

LEON. It's on your front door. *Your* name is Zubritsky.

DOCTOR. (*With profound insight.*) Wait a minute! That means that the young man in the curse may possibly be related—to our front door. (*He and* LENYA *walk over to the door, open it and look out.*)

LEON. (*To the audience.*) Mind you, I'm dealing with the intelligentsia now! . . . I continue; "The young girl's name was Sophia Zubritsky." (*To the* DOCTOR.) May I ask the name of your young daughter?

DOCTOR. Sophia.

LEON. Sophia? Sophia Zubritsky! The identical name of the girl in the curse over two hundred years ago.

DOCTOR. I can't believe it. Unless our daughter has been lying about her age. (*He and* LENYA *have come back. Each stands behind a chair.*)

LEON. "The match was doomed from the start. When Sophia's educated father learned that young Casimir was illiterate, he forbade Sophia ever to see Casimir again. Six months later Sophia married a young student, and that winter Casimir, distraught and despondent, took his life by plowing his own grave and planting himself in it. Upon hearing of his son's death, Casimir's father, Vladimir Yousekevitch—"

THE ZUBRITSKYS. (*Shaking the chairs.*) Tremble, tremble, tremble, tremble.

LEON. "—Casimir's father, Vladimir Yousekevitch—"

THE ZUBRITSKYS. Tremble, tremble, tremble, tremble.

LEON. "—Casimir's father, Vladimir Yousekevitch—"

THE ZUBRITDKYS. Tremble, tremble, tremble, tremble.

LEON. "—who caused people to tremble at the mention of his name—"

LENYA. Next time don't mention his name.

LEON. "—Casimir's father, Vla—"

THE ZUBRITSKYS. (*With a short chair shake.*) Trem—

LEON. "—and So-and-So, sometimes known as the Sorcerer because of his ability to summon the powers of the Devil himself, brought all his wrath and fury down upon Kulyenchikov . . ."

DOCTOR. Here it comes! Here it comes!

LEON. "'A curse! A curse upon all who dwell in Kulyenchikov!' he cried out. 'May the daughter of

Mikhail Zubritsky, murderer of my only son, be struck down by the ignorance that caused my son's death! May stupidity engulf her brain! May incompetence encumber her faculties! May common sense become uncommon and may reason become unreasonable!! May her children be cursed as well. And may all their children be cursed for eternity! May all who live in Kulyenchikov be born in ignorance and die in ignorance, unable to leave this cursed village until my final vengeance has been satisfied!'"

LENYA. That would explain why the train doesn't stop here.

LEON. (*To the audience.*) My initial impulse was to panic, even my secondary impulse was to panic . . . To educate is one thing, to break curses is another.

DOCTOR. Excuse me, but are you all right, Master Tolchinsky?

LEON. Yes. I'm fine. I—I was just thinking.

DOCTOR. Lenya . . . he was thinking.

LENYA. He was thinking.

DOCTOR. (*To* LEON.) What's it like?

LEON. You mean you don't know what thinking is?

DOCTOR. I don't and she certainly doesn't.

LEON. *Thinking?* It's the thoughts that come to one's mind. It's the process which enables us to make decisions.

DOCTOR. Decisions? No. I don't think we're capable of that.

LEON. But surely you know what it is you want.

LENYA. Oh, dear God, yes. We desperately want someone to help us. Not so much for us, we've already lived our lives. But for your child, our sweet daughter, Sophia.

LEON. Did you hear what you just said?

LENYA. No, I wasn't listening.

LEON. It was a decision. You decided to help your daughter because you thought about it. You are capable of thought. You think.

LENYA. No, I don't think so. It just came out.

LEON. Yes. Out of your head where your brain is lodged. The center of thoughts. And if it's possible to have even one tiny infinitesimal insignificant thought, then it's possible to expand those thoughts to ideas—and ideas into comprehension—comprehension into creativity—and finally, supreme *intelligence*!!

DOCTOR. Would I be able to open up jars? I have terrible trouble opening up jars.

LEON. (*Aside.*) Be firm, Leon. Be staunch . . . (*To the* DOCTOR.) Patience! We will break this curse, I promise you! By the simple, everyday, painstaking work of education. We must begin at once. I should like to start by seeing your daughter, Sophia.

DOCTOR. Sophia?

LEON. Yes, it occurs to me that since the curse started with the young Sophia two hundred years ago, perhaps the key to ending it lies with her direct descendant. Can I see Sophia?

LENYA. Not from here. She's up in her room. We would have to send for her.

DOCTOR. Do what the schoolmaster asks.

LENYA. She may be taking her singing lesson now.

LEON. She takes singing lessons? From whom?

LENYA. A canary. He does the best he can.

DOCTOR. No words, mind you. Just the tunes.

LEON. I understand. The girl, madame. Please.

DOCTOR. (*To* LENYA.) Remember, sweetheart, upstairs and to the left. (*She goes. To* LEON.) You'll find her a most delicate and sensitive girl. Not like the others in the village. She has so many interests, always occupied.

LEON. Occupied with what?

DOCTOR. Oh, she likes to do interesting things . . . like touching things — wood, paper, metal. She likes drinking water.

(LENYA *returns.*)

LENYA. Master Tolchinsky. May I present our daughter . . . (*She looks at piece of paper in her hand to remind her of* SOPHIA'S *name.*) Sophia Irena Elynya Zubritsky. (SOPHIA *enters.*) Sophia, this is the new schoolmaster, Leon Tolchinsky.

LEON. Miss Zubritsky! (*He turns aside, dazed.*) Is that my breath that has just been taken away? Is that vision before me human or have I too been cast under the spell? Never have I felt such a stirring beneath my breast . . . Watch yourself, Leon! She is your pupil, not the object of your dormant feelings of passion. (*He turns back to them.*) Excuse me.

DOCTOR. Do you know what he was just doing, Sophia? He was *thinking*! Isn't that wonderful?

SOPHIA. Yes, Mama.

DOCTOR. Papa! She is Mama and I am Papa.

LEON. Won't you please sit down, Miss Zubritsky? (*She sits slowly, carefully, and when she is down, the* DOCTOR *embraces* LENYA *and says, "She did it! She did it!," then turns to* LEON.)

DOCTOR. Wasn't that a beautiful sit?

LEON. Yes. Very nice. Lovely. (*To* SOPHIA.) Miss Zubritsky — may I call you Sophia?

SOPHIA. Sophia?

DOCTOR. It's your name, sweetheart.

LENYA. Say "Yes," darling. Say, "Yes, you may call me Sophia."

LEON. Please, madame. We must allow the girl to speak for herself. (*To* SOPHIA.) I should like very much to be your friend. Would it please you if I called you Sophia? (SOPHIA *looks puzzled.*)

DOCTOR. It's been so long since she's taken a test.

LEON. I think she wants to say something.

SOPHIA. I—I would be very pleased to have you call me Sophia.

DOCTOR. There you are!

LENYA. I'm so proud. So proud!

LEON. Please. It's very distracting to the girl's concentration. (*To* SOPHIA.) I've come a very long way to help you with you education. I have every reason to believe that under ordinary circumstances, you have the capability of being an extremely bright and intelligent young woman, that deep inside you somewhere is an intellect just crying to be heard, that you have enormous powers of reason. But someone has put a cloud over these powers and it is my intention to remove this cloud so that enlightenment can once more shine through those unbelievably crystal-clear blue eyes once again . . . But I need your help, Sophia. Will you give me that help?

SOPHIA. Yes. You may call me Sophia.

DOCTOR. She did it again. That's two in a row.

LEON. (*Aside.*) Get a grip, Leon. Nothing in life comes easy . . . (*To* SOPHIA.) I should like to ask you a few very simple questions. If we are to begin your education, it is important that I know at what point to begin. It won't be taxing, I promise you. I would never want to be the cause of a furrow or frown on that fair face . . . Now, then—what is your favorite color?

SOPHIA. My favorite color?

LEON. Yes, is it red or blue or green or orange? Any color at all. Which one is your favorite?

DOCTOR. I used to know that one.

LEON. I'll ask you once again, Sophia. What-is-your-favorite-color?

LENYA. Why is he being so hard on her? This isn't a university.

SOPHIA. My favorite color —

LEON. Yes?

SOPHIA. — is yellow.

LEON. Yellow! Her favorite color is yellow! Why, Sophia? Why is yellow your favorite color?

SOPHIA. Because it doesn't stick to your fingers as much.

LENYA. (*Aside, to the* DOCTOR.) I think she's wrong. I think it's blue that doesn't stick to your fingers as much.

LEON. That's a very interesting answer, Sophia. There is a certain logic to her response. The fact that that logic escapes me completely doesn't alter the fact that she has something in mind. Sophia, I'm going to ask you something quite simple now. I'm going to ask you to make a wish. Do you know what a wish is?

SOPHIA. Yes. A wish is something you hope for that doesn't come true.

LEON. Well, perhaps we can change all that. If you could make a wish that did come true, anything at all, what would you wish for?

SOPHIA. What would I wish for?

LEON. Yes, Sophia, what would you wish for?

SOPHIA. I would wish that I could fly like a bird . . . to soar over buildings and trees . . . to float on the wind and be carried far away . . . over mountains and lakes

. . . over forests and rivers . . . to meet people in other villages . . . to see what the world was like . . . to know all the things that I shall never know because I must always remain here in this place.

LEON. Sophia, that is the most beautiful wish I have ever heard. (*To the* ZUBRITSKYS.) Don't you see what her wish means? To fly like a bird means to sever the bonds that chain her to ignorance. She wants to soar, to grow, she wants knowledge! And with every fiber of my being, from the very depths of my soul, I shall gather all my strength and patience and dedication, and I make this promise that I, Leon Steponovitch Tolchinsky, shall make Sophia Zubritsky's wish come true.

SOPHIA. If you could do that, schoolmaster, I would be in your debt — forever.

LEON. She touches me so. Your daughter has such a sweet soul and such a pure heart. We must begin as soon as possible. Not another moment must be lost. I shall return in the morning at eight o'clock sharp. (*To* SOPHIA.) What subject shall we begin our studies with, Sophia?

SOPHIA. I should like to begin with — languages.

LEON. Languages! Of course! Even I should have thought of that. Languages it shall be, my dear, sweet Sophia . . . And what language shall we begin with first?

SOPHIA. (*Thinks.*) Rabbit, I think.

LEON. *Rabbit*?

DOCTOR. A very hard language, rabbit. Hardly anyone speaks it anymore.

LENYA. As long as she gets a few phrases, it's enough to bagin with.

SOPHIA. Am I through for today?

LEON. Yes.

SOPHIA. Then I shall go to my room.

LENYA. Watch how she gets up from the chair. Watch! You didn't see it. Sophia, do it again.

LEON. It's not necessary. She's already past getting up from chairs.

DOCTOR. They're so much smarter than in our day.

SOPHIA. Until tomorrow, schoolmaster.

LEON. In all my life, I have never looked forward to a morning as much as tomorrow's.

SOPHIA. I think you are the most beautiful schoolteacher I have ever seen, Master Tolchinsky. I pray that you don't despair of Kulyenchikov . . . and that you will stay with us forever. (*She leaves.*)

LENYA. She found the door! She found the door!

DOCTOR. I've never seen Sophia so radiant . . . Lenya, are you thinking what I'm thinking?

LENYA. I'm not even thinking what *I'm* thinking. What are you talking about?

DOCTOR. I think our Sophia has taken a liking to the new schoolmaster.

LEON. If it is true, Dr. Zubritsky, then standing before you is the happiest man on the happiest planet in the universe. Tell me, is she spoken for?

DOCTOR. Spoken for?

LEON. Does she have any suitors? Any young men desperately in love with her?

DOCTOR. We—we don't talk of such things.

LEON. Why not?

DOCTOR. There is no one. No one at all. Not even *him*.

LEON. *Him*?

LENYA. He didn't mean him. He meant someone else who isn't him.

LEON. There is someone. Who is it? I must know. It's of the greatest concern to me.

DOCTOR. If I told you who him was, you must promise never to say it was I who told you it was him.

LEON. I promise.

DOCTOR. Have you ever heard of . . . Count Gregor of Kulyenchikov?

LEON. I can't say that I have.

DOCTOR. You can't say that? It's not that hard. Even Lenya can say that.

LENYA. Count Gregor of Kul—

LEON. (*Annoyed.*) Yes! Yes! I can say it. Who is he?

LENYA. He's—he's one of them. The ones who put the purse on us.

LEON. You mean—a Yousekevitch?

DOCTOR. The last of his line.

LEON. Tell me about him and Sophia.

DOCTOR. He proposes marriage twice a day.

LEON. Twice a day?

LENYA. Six-fifteen in the mornings, seven-twenty at nights.

LEON. He cares for her that much?

DOCTOR. He cares only about avenging his ancestors. If a Zubritsky marries a Yousekevitch, they will be satisfied and the nurse will be over.

LEON. Does Sophia care for him?

DOCTOR. She has said no for many years, but she can't resist much longer. The poor girl wants to sleep late just one morning.

LEON. What kind of a man is this Count Yousekevitch?

LENYA. You know . . . like the rest of us.

LEON. You mean he is cursed as well?

DOCTOR. He still lives in Kulyenchikov. He's not permitted to leave here either.

LEON. I understand. If I have a rival, I am more

determined than ever to break this curse. God bless you both for your faith in me. Tomorrow the education of Sophia Zubritsky begins. In all my excitement, I forgot to ask. What about lodgings?

DOCTOR. Oh, don't worry about it. We'll be very comfortable right here.

LEON. Of course. I'll see you in the morning.

LENYA. Master Tolchinsky! Please! Ask us again! Ask us the question. It makes us feel . . . important.

LEON. Yes, certainly. What is the purpose of man's existence?

LENYA. I'm all choked up again. I'm sorry I asked.

DOCTOR. One moment! I—I think I know. I think I know the answer.

LEON. To the purpose of man's existence?

LENYA. What are you talking about?

DOCTOR. It's true. The first time I heard it I didn't understand. But now, suddenly something came to me. I know my limitations, but still, I think I really know the answer . . . Oh, my God, what if I'm right?

LEON. (*Excitedly.*) Tell me, Dr. Zubritsky. Tell me what you think the answer is.

DOCTOR. I think—it's *twelve!*

LEON. *Twelve?*

DOCTOR. It's wrong; I can tell by your face. Fourteen?

LEON. I think you missed the point.

DOCTOR. It's less than a hundred, I know that. Even *I'm* not that stupid. Eighty-three . . . forty-six.

LEON. (*Moving on.*) We'll discuss it when we get to philosophy. Don't think about it. Get some sleep. Good night. Until tomorrow. (*He walks out to the street and screams.*) TWELVE?

LENYA. Why didn't you leave well enough alone? Why must you have answers? Aren't questions beautiful enough?

LEON. (*In the street.*) TWELVE!

DOCTOR. But what if I am right? I could have sold the answer. We could have made a fortune. (*They leave . . . the set goes off.* LEON *reappears.*)

LEON. (*To the audience.*) That's it. I'm leaving now, so I'll say goodbye. I *was* going to stay and try to break the curse, but when he siad "Twelve," I knew it was time to go . . . What I must do now is try to forget Sophia. I must!

SOPHIA'S VOICE. Schoolmaster!

LEON. Sophia? Where are you?

(*She appears on the balcony.*)

SOPHIA. Down here. I had to see you once more.

LEON. Without a wrap? In the cold night air, you'll come down with a chill.

SOPHIA. Oh, I never catch colds.

LEON. You don't.

SOPHIA. I've tried. I've just never learned how to do it.

LEON. Be grateful . . . Some things are not worth knowing.

SOPHIA. I know that something has happened a long time ago that prevents me from knowing what happened a long time ago. If only you knew me the way I might have been instead of the way I am.

LEON. But if you were not the way you are, then I would not have come here to help you to become the way you might have been. (*Aside, quickly.*) Careful! You're beginning to think like her.

SOPHIA. Could you—could you ever care for someone who never became the way I might have been?

LEON. Could I ever care for someone who never became—I see what you mean. I see what you're getting at. Yes. Yes, I could. I would. I shall. I will. I have. I do.

SOPHIA. Is that rabbit you're speaking? It's hard to follow.

LEON. If it sounds like gibberish it's because you do that to me, Sophia. When thoughts come from the heart they sometimes trip over the tongue.

SOPHIA. Then I must watch where I walk when you speak . . . I must go. Everything depends upon tomorrow.

LEON. And if not tomorrow, then the tomorrow after tomorrow. And all the tomorrows for the rest of my life, if that's what it takes.

SOPHIA. No. It all rests on tomorrow. If we fail, we shall never see each other again.

LEON. Never see each other? What do you mean?

SOPHIA. I never know what I mean. I do have thoughts but they seem to disappear when they reach my lips.

LEON. If I ever reached your lips, I would never disappear.

SOPHIA. Would you like to kiss me?

LEON. With all my heart.

SOPHIA. No. I meant with your lips.

LEON. An even better suggestion.

SOPHIA. Hurry. Hurry.

(*He climbs up to the balcony.*)

LEON. I'm climbing as fast as I can.

(*She disappears.*)

LEON. (*Arrives on the balcony.*) Where are you?

SOPHIA. (*Appears below.*) Up here.

LEON. (*To the audience.*) If only she were ugly, I'd be halfway home by now. (*To* SOPHIA.) Stay where you are. I'll come to you.

SOPHIA. All right. (*But he doesn't move.*)

LEON. (*To the audience.*) After a while you get the hang of it.

SOPHIA. (*Reappears on the balcony.*) Here I am.

LEON. My kiss, sweet Sophia. (*They kiss.*)

SOPHIA. As we kissed I felt a strange flutter in my heart.

LEON. So did I.

SOPHIA. You felt a flutter in my heart as well? How alike we are. And yet your hair is so much shorter . . . I must go. I'm about to fall asleep and I want to get to bed in time. (*She leaves.*)

LEON. (*To the audience.*) I know the dangers of loving such a simple soul. It would mean a lifetime of sweet, blissful passion — and very short conversations at breakfast. (*There is a clap of thunder.*) I'd best find some comfortable lodgings. (*He descends. There is another clap of thunder.*)

SCENE 4

SNETSKY. (*Running onstage.*) Was that you?

LEON. I beg your pardon?

SNETSKY. Were you responsible for making that dreadful noise?

LEON. Of course not. That was thunder and lightning. It's caused by extreme atmospheric pressures in the skies above us.

SNETSKY. Well, whoever did it is going to get Count Yousekevitch very angry at us.

LEON. Count Yousekevitch?

SNETSKY. He's the one who lives in the big house on

top of the hill. Every time he hears someone make that
noise, he throws water down on us.

LEON. No, no, Snetsky, that's rain. Rain!

(YENCHNA *appears. She carries flowers.*)

YENCHNA. Umbrellas! Umbrellas for sale! Get your
umbrellas before he throws the water.

LEON. Yenchna, no one throws water. It's rain from
the skies caused by a buildup of condensed moisture.

YENCHNA. You can tell that to these fools, but I used
to be a substitute teacher . . . Umbrellas!

LEON. Excuse me, but would either one of you know
of a place to stay?

(SLOVITCH *appears with* MISHKIN.)

SLOVITCH. What's going on? What's all the racket?

MISHKIN. I knew it. I knew he would throw water
down on us today. Every time I wash my cow, you know
he's going to throw water.

LEON. Mishkin, would you happen to know—
(*Prelude chimes, which precede the actual ringing of
the steeple bell.*)

SLOVITCH. Oh-oh. It's time for Count Yousekevitch to
propose again.

MISHKIN. This could be the day. One yes from her
and we could all be smart again.

LEON. You mean you want Sophia to marry him?

SNETSKY. Not unless she wanted to. But it would be
nice to remember my first name.

LEON. But that's a terrible sacrifice to ask of Sophia.
Surely you wouldn't ask that of her.

YENCHNA. What kind of sacrifice? To live in a big

house up on the hill . . . To have little macaroons whenever you want . . . To have a maid brush your teeth in the morning . . .

LEON. But does she love him?

SNETSKY. I beg your pardon?

LEON. Does she love him?

SLOVITCH. We don't have any.

LEON. You don't have any what?

SLOVITCH. Love! It's part of the curse.

LEON. I don't understand.

MISHKIN. I hear him coming. You'd better leave, schoolmaster. He doesn't like people around. (SLOVITCH, MISHKIN *and* SNETSKY *leave.*)

LEON. Yenchna! Is it true there is no love in Kulyenchikov?

YENCHNA. I wouldn't know. My late husband's been gone almost fourteen years.

LEON. I'm sorry.

YENCHNA. That's a long time to be late. I wish he was dead. (*She leaves.*)

LEON. I'm breaking out in a cold sweat. The possibility of losing Sophia terrifies me . . . I'm going to eavesdrop. (*He hides begind a tree.*)

GREGOR. (*Offstage.*) Sophia! (*Strumming a balalaika,* GREGOR YOUSEKEVITCH *appears.*) Sweet Sophia! Time to wake up, my pretty one . . . time to get proposed to. She's asleep! Perhaps a pebble will awaken her. (*He picks up a pebble and tosses it up to the balcony. We hear a crash of glass.* DR. ZUBRITSKY *appears in a nightshirt, holding a candle.*)

DOCTOR. Who did that?

GREGOR. It is I, Count Yousekevitch.

DOCTOR. Good evening, sir. (*He bows and knocks his head on the railing.*)

GREGOR. I've come to propose.

DOCTOR. Well, you're a little late. I'm married almost twenty-six years.

LENYA. (*Offstage.*) Nikolai! Nikolai!

DOCTOR. I'm out here, Lenya. What did you want?

(LENYA *appears. She holds a lit candle.*)

LENYA. Some bandages. My feet are bleeding . . . who are you talking to?

GREGOR. It is I, Madame Zubritsky. Count Yousekevitch. I've come to propose to Sophia.

LENYA. She's busy throwing water on the drapes. They're on fire.

DOCTOR. The drapes are on fire?

LENYA. I had to light something . . . I couldn't find my candle.

(SOPHIA *comes out.*)

SOPHIA. Papa, what's going on?

DOCTOR. Did we wake you, darling?

SOPHIA. No. I was reading by the light of the drapes.

GREGOR. I must be crazy marrying into this family.

DOCTOR. Count Yousekevitch wants to propose to you, darling. Go ahead, Count Yousekevitch.

GREGOR. Can't we be alone?

DOCTOR. No. No. I think Sophia should hear this, too.

GREGOR. Very well. Will you marry me, Sophia?

LENYA. Oh, my God, this is so romantic. I just wish my feet weren't bleeding.

SOPHIA. I'm sorry, Coung Yousekevitch, but marriage is a very great step to take and I don't wish to make it while I do not have the intelligence to know what I am stepping into. Good night, sir. Good night, Mama, good night, Papa.

LENYA. Good night, son. When you're through reading, darling, put out the drapes.

GREGOR. I do not give up easily. I'll be back in the morning.

DOCTOR. Good night, your grace.

LENYA. Good night, Grace. (*They bow low.*)

DOCTOR. Watch what you're doing, you're burning my mustache.

GREGOR. (*Aside.*) Having them for in-laws in a curse worse than the curse.

LEON. Pray God it never happens.

GREGOR. Who's that? Who's there? Come out, I say!

LEON. Forgive me, sir. I was just passing by. May I introduce myself. I am—

GREGOR. I know who you are. You're the new schoolmaster who has come here in a pathetic attempt to break the curse of Kulyenchikov.

LEON. As I have just witnessed your pathetic attempt to win Sophia.

GREGOR. Everyone's a critic. The curse can only be broken if you can educate her, which you can't . . . or if she marries me.

LEON. Which apparently she won't. Why don't you pursue some other girl?

GREGOR. Because Sophia is beautiful. Did you ever see the other girls in the village? They look like me!

LEON. For a man so powerful, you seem to have an inordinate lack of self-esteem. I am sorry for you. Good day, sir.

GREGOR. Not *good* day. *One* day.

LEON. I beg your pardon?

GREGOR. Were you not aware that if at the end of one brief day you have not succeeded to raise her intellect you must be gone from our village? To remain for even one second past the allotted time means you will fall victim to the curse yourself. (*To the audience.*) I love that part.

LEON. I cannot believe such nonsense. Threaten me all you want, sir, but I will never leave. To be quite honest, I love Sophia Zubritsky.

GREGOR. Love??? There is no love in Kulyenchikov. It's all part of the curse.

LEON. You mean Sophia cannot love me?

GREGOR. You have one day to find that out, sir. One single day. Twenty-five measly hours.

LEON. Twenty-four.

GREGOR. What?

LEON. There are twenty-four hours in a day.

GREGOR. I believe you are thinking of February, sir. Good night. (*He leaves.*)

LEON. But is it true? If I cannot teach Sophia to think in twenty-four hours, she will never be able to love me?

(SOPHIA *appears on the balcony.*)

SOPHIA. Leon!

LEON. Sophia! Are you all right?

SOPHIA. I must talk to you. Someplace where we'll not be seen.

LEON. Wherever you say.

SOPHIA. Can you meet me here?

LEON. Yes. When?

SOPHIA. Now!

LEON. Now? Yes. Of course. That's where I am.

SOPHIA. Come up here. Hurry, Leon, hurry. It's of

the utmost importance. I overheard your conversation
with the Count. (*He climbs up to the balcony.*) Leon, I
cannot be taught. You must leave Kulyenchikov at
once.

LEON. Never without you.

SOPHIA. Then take me with you. Tonight.

LEON. But the curse—

SOPHIA. It cannot be broken. But we can live in the
swamp and eat brown roots and I will become old and
ugly and more stupid and more ignorant and never love
you but at least we'll be together.

LEON. Well, that wasn't exactly what I had in mind.

SOPHIA. Then we are lost.

LEON. No, no, Sophia. I will teach you. I will break
this curse. Tomorrow, I promise you.

SOPHIA. Oh, Leon, I wish I could love you.

LEON. You will, Sophia. Tomorrow. I promise.

SOPHIA. Until tomorrow. (*She goes inside. He climbs
down.*)

LEON. I wish she'd sleep in the kitchen.

(SOPHIA *reappears.*)

SOPHIA. Leon! Come back! Hurry, hurry.

(*He climbs back up.*)

LEON. What is it?

SOPHIA. I couldn't sleep. I'm so frightened.

LEON. Don't be frightened, Sophia.

SOPHIA. If I could know the feeling of loving you
for just one day, I would endure a hundred thousand
years of curses . . . Good night, Leon. God bless you
and keep you. (*She leaves.*)

LEON. (*To the audience.*) She asks not to *be* loved but to know what it means to give her love to another. I think I have wandered into a very special place. I love Yenchna, I love Snetsky and Mishkin, and yes, even Coung Yousekevitch. *All* of them. God give me the strength to break this curse — and to get up and down this balcony. (*He gets down.*) By the way, I urge you to give the matter some thought yourselves. I have no wish to alarm you, but you are, after all, sitting within the bounds of Kulyenchikov. Therefore, I wish us both the best of luck. (*He starts to leave.*)

SOPHIA. (*Reappears on the balcony.*) Leon! I forgot to tell you something!

LEON. (*Gasping.*) Tomorrow, Sophia! I can't *take* any more news tonight! (*He walks off, clutching his chest.*)

CURTAIN

Act Two

Scene 1

The town square, early next morning. A rooster crows. SNETSKY *appears and yawns in unison with crowing.* SLOVITCH *comes out of his shop.*

SNETSKY. Slovitch, any news?

SLOVITCH. About what?

SNETSKY. About what? About the curse, of course. Has it been lifted yet?

SLOVITCH. How would I know?

SNETSKY. Let's see if there's anything in the newspaper.

SLOVITCH. Good idea. It rained during the night.

SNETSKY. Where does it say that?

SLOVITCH. I can feel it. The paper's all damp.

SNETSKY. Maybe your dog did that.

SLOVITCH. No, no. He's housebroken. He only does it inside. (YENCHNA *appears, pulling a cow that is upside down.*) What's wrong with your cow?

YENCHNA. He's tired. I've been milking him since four o'clock.

SLOVITCH. Upside down?

YENCHNA. You get a little more cream that way? (*She starts to leave.*) Cream! Fresh cream right from the top. Drink it right from the spigot, two kopecks a mouthful! Fresh cream . . . right from the udder. (*She is gone. We move to the* DOCTOR'S *house. He and* LENYA *appear, carrying lit candles.*)

DOCTOR. Come. Let us pray, Lenya. Pray for deliverance. Dear Lord, who art in heaven. We art in Kulyenchikov, and we art in trouble. (*They are on their knees in front of the sofa.*)

45

LENYA. We art a simple people, dear Lord.

DOCTOR. But we're not so simple that we don't believe in you.

LENYA. Forgive us our sins, dear Lord.

DOCTOR. We know not what we do because we know not what we do.

BOTH. God bless us, God bless our daughter, God bless the schoolmaster and God bless yourself, whoever you are. Amen.

(*There is a knock.*)

DOCTOR. Was that the door?

LENYA. No, I think it was someone knocking.

DOCTOR. Well, open it, open it! It must be the schoolmaster. (*He calls out.*) Sophia! It's time. Wake up! Give yourself a nudge. (*To* LENYA, *as* LENYA *pushes against the door.*) The other way! The other way!

(LEON *enters, breathless.*)

LEON. Do you know what time it is?

DOCTOR. Ten to six?

LENYA. Eight-fifteen?

DOCTOR. A quarter to nine?

LENYA. We don't have a clock.

DOCTOR. Pick any one you want. Ten-twenty, eleven-forty. Is there something in there you like?

LEON. You don't understand. The Count said I had only twenty-four hours to break the curse after I arrived in Kulyenchikov. I arrived yesterday morning at exactly nine o'clock. It's eight o'clock now. That means I have only one hour. It doens't even *leave* me one hour. I've just used up an entire minute telling you how much time

I haven't got left . . . Dear God, help me. Help me, dear Lord.

DOCTOR. What a shame. You just missed him. We finished services two minutes ago.

LEON. Get Sophia! We can't lose another moment. Hurry, I beg of you.

(*We hear footsteps.*)

DOCTOR. Listen! I hear footsteps coming down the stairs.

(SOPHIA *rushes in.*)

SOPHIA. Good morning, Mama. Good morning, Papa. Good morning, schoolmaster.

DOCTOR. She got all three right! This is going to be her day, I know it!

LEON. And looking more radiant than ever.

LENYA. Where shall we sit?

LEON. Doctor, with all due respect, I need Sophia's full concentration this morning. I must ask the parents to leave the room.

DOCTOR. By all means. We'll see that you're not disturbed. Goodbye, Sophia.

(LENYA *and the* DOCTOR *walk over to the door.*)

LENYA. Goodbye, my little angel.

DOCTOR. Do as the schoolmaster tells you.

LENYA. We'll be praying for you every minute.

DOCTOR. If you succeed, schoolmaster, give us the signal by rapping on the window three times, followed by too short ones —

LENYA. — followed by six long ones.

DOCTOR. If you fail, rap seven times quickly —

LENYA. — followed by three times slowly.

DOCTOR. If you want lunch —

LEON. *Will you please leave!* (*He gently pushes them out.*)

BOTH. We're going! We're going! (*They are on the other side of the closed door.*)

LENYA. Something's not right, I can feel it in my bones.

DOCTOR. He can hear you. Lower your voice.

(LENYA *bends her knees, lowering herself.*)

LENYA. I'm a mother. I know about these things. Why do you look taller to me lately? (*They exit.*)

LEON. Sophia . . . Last night I decided that the task before us is one step beyond impossible. I knew I would fail and that I had to leave Kulyenchikov, like all those who have failed before me, . . . but today, looking into your eyes, I know there is no life for me without you. Therefore, we must not think of failure, we cannot afford to despair. Only a miracle can save us, Sophia, but with a majestic, supreme effort, we must try to make that miracle happen.

SOPHIA. What is a miracle?

LEON. A miracle is a wish that God makes. You are a miracle, Sophia.

SOPHIA. You mean God wished for me?

LEON. In one of his most sublime moments . . . We must hurry, Sophia. (*He picks up a book.*) This is a primary book of mathematics. It's used to teach very small children very simple problems in arithmetic.

SOPHIA. Do you think it's too advanced for me?

LEON. I don't think so, Sophia. We can't go back any

further than this book. Now, let us begin . . . (*He opens the book to the first page. A large number one fills up the page.*) One is the figure, the word, the symbol for a single item. One finger, one Sophia, one Leon, one book . . . Now then, I am holding up one finger, Sophia. Now I am holding up a second finger. One plus one is two. Would you repeat that for me, Sophia.

SOPHIA. Which part?

LEON. One—

SOPHIA. One.

LEON. Plus one—

SOPHIA. Plus one.

LEON. Is Two!

SOPHIA. Is two!

LEON. Yes! Yes! Yes! Wonderful. We're making headway. Slow, invisible headway . . . I'm very, very proud of you, Sophia. Are we ready to go on?

SOPHIA. Yes. History, please. I hope I can master it as well as I have mathematics.

LEON. Well, I honestly don't think we've conquered mathematics yet. There are problems that could come up. Let's continue. One plus two is three.

SOPHIA. Am I finished with one plus one?

LEON. You are if you remember the answer.

SOPHIA. I remembered it before. Is it necessary to remember it again?

LEON. Of course it's necessary to remember it again. It's necessary to remember if for *always*.

SOPHIA. You mean you will always be asking me what one plus one is?

LEON. No! Once you tell me, we can move on to other things. Like one plus two and one plus three, and so on. But if you can't remember what one plus one is, then the answer to one plus two is meaningless.

SOPHIA. Do you know how much one plus one is?

LEON. Certainly.

SOPHIA. Then why is it necessary for me to know? Certainly, if you have such esteem and affection for me, you will tell me the answer whenever I ask you.

LEON. But I won't always be around to tell you. You have to know for yourself. In case other people ask you.

SOPHIA. No one here ever asks questions like that. Even if I told them, they wouldn't know if it was the right answer.

LEON. Becuase they are cursed with ignorance. And we are trying to lift that debilitating affliction.

SOPHIA. You're getting angry with me. What's the point of being educated if you get angry? When you didn't ask me such questions, you always said the loveliest things to me. Is this what it's like to be intelligent?

LEON. No, Sophia. It is I who am not being intelligent. It's frustration and impatience that drives me to such crude behavior. Forgive me. We'll start from the beginning again. One plus one is two. Repeat.

SOPHIA. One plus one is two. Repeat.

LEON. *No!!* Don't repeat the word "repeat." Just repeat the part before I say "repeat" . . . Now watch me carefully: One plus one is two. *Repeat!!*

SOPHIA. What were you like as a little boy?

LEON. (*Angrily.*) What was I like as a little boy?

SOPHIA. You're shouting again.

LEON. (*Tries to placate her.*) I was inquisitive. Probing. Wondering why we were put on this earth and what the purpose of man's existence was.

SOPHIA. The purpose of man's existence . . . !

LEON. (*Shouts.*) *I've had enough of that.* Sophia, you must stop asking me questions. Our time is nearly gone.

SOPHIA. Then how am I to learn?

LEON. Sophia, you must answer what I ask, not what you want me to answer.

SOPHIA. Then I will learn only what *you* want me to know. Why can't I learn what I want to know?

LEON. Because what you want to know is of no practical value. What I want to teach is acceptable knowledge.

SOPHIA. Is knowing what you were like as a little boy not acceptable knowledge?

LEON. Of course not. It's of no significance at all.

SOPHIA. But it's much more interesting than that which is significant.

LEON. But I'm not trying to interest you. I'm trying to educate you.

SOPHIA. I know. But while you fail to educate me, you never fail to interest me. I find that very significant.

LEON. There is nothing like the logic of an illogical mind! Let's try one more time.

(*The* DOCTOR *and* LENYA *appear outside.* LENYA *peers through the transom.*)

DOCTOR. She must be speaking rabbit like a bunny by now.

(SLOVITCH *comes out of his shop.*)

SLOVITCH. How much longer is this going to take? I haven't sold a sausage all morning.

(MISHKIN *appears.*)

MISHKIN. Good morning, Dr. Zubritsky.
DOCTOR. (*To* LENYA.) What's going on?

(LEON *is on the floor banging his head in dismay.*)

LENYA. I think he's teaching her gymnastics.

MISHKIN. Dr. Zubritsky, I have an urgent letter for schoolmaster Tolchinsky.

DOCTOR. Quiet, please. This is a school zone.

(YENCHNA *and* SNETSKY *appear.*)

MISHKIN. I have an important letter for him. It's marked urgent, so I only went to three wrong houses first.

DOCTOR. Can't you see he's busy? Bring it back later.

LENYA. I don't like the way it's going. I just don't like the way it's going.

DOCTOR. Let us pray. Let us all pray to the Lord that this young man will deliver us from bondage. Let us ask for his blessing. Very religious on this side, semireligious on the other . . . (LEON *comes out.*) Quiet! Quiet, everyone! The schoolmaster wants to speak . . . Please, God, let this be the answer to our prayers.

SNETSKY. Ah-men!

LENYA AND YENCHNA. Ah women!

DOCTOR. (*To* LEON.) Is my daughter—you know—empty or full?

LEON. She is the same as always. I have only moments and I must ask this quickly, because I may not have the intelligence to ask this later. Because of my deep and unbounded devotion for your daughter, Sophia, I would like to ask for her hand in marriage. I ask this of you now while I still love her. In a few minutes I may not know the meaning of the word. When the clock in the church steeple strikes nine, I hope you will have an answer for me. (*He goes back inside.*)

DOCTOR. He's a nice young man. I'll say that. Very ambitious. Lenya, what do you think?

LENYA. If the man can't break a simple curse, how's he going to put bread on the table?

MISHKIN. And what about Tremble?

DOCTOR. Who?

MISHKIN. Tremble Tremble. You know, up on the hill. The one who throws the water.

SNETSKY. Mishkin's right. It's his curse. He would never permit such a marriage.

MISHKIN. Wait! There is one chance. If a stranger marries a Kulyenchikovite before he becomes like us, then he is free to take her away from here.

DOCTOR. I didn't know that.

MISHKIN. It was added to the curse two years ago . . . to make it more exciting.

SLOVITCH. You would never see your daughter again, but you would know she was happy and getting smarter every day.

SNETSKY. Oh, give it, Doctor. Give her your permission.

YENCHNA. If you don't give it to her, give it to me.

DOCTOR. I don't know. It's a decision, and I can't make decisions. Let's leave it to God. Let God make the decision.

(*They get on their knees and pray.*)

SOPHIA. What are you doing, Leon?

(LEON *sits, musing.*)

LEON. Having my last thoughts. One final pleasurable moment of reason.

SOPHIA. Then I was right. A wish is something you hope for that doesn't come true.

LEON. I'm sorry. I cannot help you soar over mountains and lakes, Sophia. But I will not leave you. I will remain here for the rest of my days, not basking in the light of your beauty but cowering in the darkness of my own ignorance . . . for that is the measure of my esteem and affection for you.

SOPHIA. I would do anything to save you from this calamity . . . anything! (*Prelude chimes.*) Oh, run, Leon. Run for your life. There are ignorant girls in other villages you could learn to love.

LEON. Listen to me carefully and remember it forever. I love you with all my heart.

(*The bells begin.*)

SNETSKY. Listen! The church bell!

LEON. I may never say these words again. (*Bell.*)

SLOVITCH. The time is up!

LEON. Savor it, Sophia. Keep the memeory of what I say. (*Bell.*)

YENCHNA. Her last chance to marry. I know the feeling.

LEON. The way I gaze lovingly into your eyes as I do now.

LENYA. Say it, husband. Give them permission to marry. Quickly. (*Bell.*)

LEON. All the love I would have given you in a lifetime must be compressed into a final instant. (*Bell.*)

DOCTOR. Yes. I'll give it. I'll go in there and give my permission right now.

LEON. Goodbye, sweet Sophia. I did not love you long, but I loved you well. (*Bell.*)

DOCTOR. I'll just wait to see what time it is first.

LEON. Tell everyone in Kulyenchikov that I — (*Bell. LEON freezes, a dumb look on his face.*)

MAGISTRATE. (*On the balcony.*) Nine o'clock and all's well!

(*They all rush into the house.*)

DOCTOR. Wonderful news, Master Tolchinsky!

SOPHIA. Mama! Papa! Everyone! The schoolmaster has something to say. Let us all listen . . . Leon, didn't you want to say something?

LEON. (*Bewildered, befuddled.*) Yes, but you said we should all listen.

(*The MAGISTRATE has joined them.*)

YENCHNA. Oh, oh!

SNETSKY. He's got a look on his face I've seen before.

SLOVITCH. It's the same one you've got on your face.

SOPHIA. (*To LEON.*) No, I meant that we will all listen while you tell us what you have to say.

LEON. Oh! I see . . . Thank you . . . Actually, I don't have much to say.

SNETSKY. There's no fool like a new fool.

DOCTOR. Young man, do you still want to marry my daughter?

LEON. Marry your daughter! Oh, no, sir, you do me too great an honor.

YENCHNA. I knew he'd never make it when he bought the whitefish from me.

MAGISTRATE. All right, move along. Break it up, you've all seen a ninny-poop before. Let's keep it moving. Come on.

(YENCHNA, *the* MAGISTRATE, SNETSKY *and* SLOVITCH
   leave.)

MISHKIN. (*To* LEON.) If you ever want this urgent letter, let me know. Not that anything in your life is urgent
anymore. (*He puts the letter back in his pouch and
leaves.*)

LENYA. Sophia, darling, go in the garden and plant
some vegetables. We'll have salad tonight for dinner.
(*She leaves.*)

DOCTOR. So, young man — what are your plans now
that everything has fallen apart at the top?

LEON. I'm not sure. This absense of thought will take
some getting used to

DOCTOR. Well, you might try politics. You sound very
well suited for it.

LEON. Oh, this is an old suit. If I went into politics I
would need all new clothes.

DOCTOR. This is really just one doctor's opinion, but
when you catch a curse you really catch a curse. (*To*
SOPHIA.) Don't stay up too long. I want you to go up on
the roof later and take the canary for a walk. (*He
leaves.*)

LEON. I'm sorry, Sophia. Weren't we in the middle of
a lesson when the clock began to chime? What were we
saying?

SOPHIA. You said that you loved me and that I should
savor it and keep it as a memory because soon you
would not love me ever again. Do you not love me now,
Leon?

LEON. Love you? I'm not quite sure I know what the
word means. Perhaps if you kissed me. Would you like
to?

SOPHIA. With all my heart.

LEON. No, I meant—

SOPHIA. I know what you meant. (*They kiss, warmly.*) Oh, Leon! The less you know, the better you kiss!

LEON. And the better I kiss, the more brilliant I become! Oh, my dear sweet Sophia, look at me! Look at me and tell me what you see! (*He has jumped up on the* DOCTOR's *sofa.*)

SOPHIA. I see a very good kisser dirtying my father's sofa.

LEON. No, Sophia. You see a man of intellect inspired by love. I am not cursed, Sophia. I still have my intelligence. I only pretended to be stupid.

SOPHIA. You pretended to be stupid?

LEON. Yes.

SOPHIA. That doesn't sound very intelligent to me.

LEON. It will soon, I promise.

SOPHIA. But the curse . . .

LEON. It had no effect on me. Oh, I was plenty worried, I admit. Especially when the clock struck nine. But when nothing happened, I suddenly realized—you can't be cursed unless you *permit* yourself to be. Kulyenchikov's lack of intelligence is self-inflicted, caused by fear and guilt and the relinquishing of your own self-esteem to a tyrannical power. Do you understand what I'm saying?

SOPHIA. Everything but the explanation.

LEON. If a parent tells you you are a naughty child from the day you were born, you will grow up believing you are a worthless human being. And from the day *you* were born, you were told you were all stupid. Now do you understand?

SOPHIA Not as well as before.

LEON. I know that telling it doesn't change it. You

must be shown. When I was standing there, I suddenly became inspired. I hit upon a plan that will break this curse and save you from Yousekevitch.

SOPHIA. What is it?

LEON. You must marry Yousekevitch.

SOPHIA. Are you still pretending to be stupid?

LEON. No, Sophia. I don't mean Count Gregor.

SOPHIA. Oh, thank goodness. You had me frightened half to death.

LEON. You will marry me, Sophia. I will be Yousekevitch. Do you understand?

SOPHIA. Don't ask me that question anymore.

LEON. Trust me, Sophia. The wedding will take place tomorrow. Tomorrow the curse will be over. Tomorrow you will be intelligent. Tomorrow you will love me, Sophia.

SOPHIA. Could I have a kiss just to tide me over?

LEON. Of course, my sweet. I must go set my plan in action.

SOPHIA. I'm so excited, Leon. Tonight I will clear all the nonsense out of my head to prepare for all the knowledge that will be coming in. I love rearranging things. (*She leaves.*)

LEON. (*To the audience.*) The plan begins. I must find Count Yousekevitch. (*He leaves,* YOUSEKEVITCH *appears, and addresses the audience.*)

GREGOR. Was he just talking about me? You like him, don't you? Better than me, right? Admit it . . . I would give up all my wealth and powers if I could be the hero. I wouldn't have to wear this dumb outfit . . . people would applaud when I come on. You're not even listening to me, are you? All you care about is getting those two kids together . . . I hope it's raining when you leave here. (*He starts to leave.* LEON *rushes onstage.*)

LEON. Oh, good day, Coung Yousekevitch. You remember me? Something Something Tolchinsky.

GREGOR. (*To the audience.*) Listen to this conversation. What is it, Something?

LEON. I couldn't help overhearing what you just said. I want you to know that even though I've lost most of my intelligence—

GREGOR. —all of it.

LEON. —all of it—I am not without some feelings. It pains me to know that being disliked makes you so unhappy.

GREGOR. Oh, That's easy for you to say. You don't like me either, do you?

LEON. Well, I don't dislike you.

GREGOR. But do you like me?

LEON. No. Not much.

GREGOR. You see!

LEON. Because you never do anything redeeming. Why not?

GREGOR. I don't know. I was brought up that way, I guess. My father taught me since I was a little boy, if you want to hold your power over these people, you must never be nice to them. Always make them fear and tremble.

LEON. Did you like your father?

GREGOR. Oh, he was all right, I guess.

LEON. You didn't like him, did you?

GREGOR. Don't tell anyone. When I was nine months old I tried to crawl away from home.

LEON. There you are! Then, the answer to being liked is to do something redeeming. Isn't there something good you could do for the village?

GREGOR. You mean like a barbecue?

LEON. Well, it's a start. But I was thinking of

something on a much grander scale. Like lifting the curse.

GREGOR. How can I? It won't be lifted unless Sophia marries me.

LEON. Or another Yousekevitch.

GREGOR. There is none. I'm the last of the line.

LEON. Unless you had a son.

GREGOR. But I'm not even married. I may be a villain, but I don't fool around. Maybe that's why I'm so unhappy.

LEON. You don't have to be married. You can adopt a son.

GREGOR. Adopt a son? Who?

LEON. Me!

GREGOR. You?

LEON. I'm single, available, ready and willing. I'm not very intelligent but I will be once the curse is lifted.

GREGOR. I've always wanted a son. Someone to take on fishing trips.

LEON. I never really had a father.

GREGOR. My boy, Leon. I'd spoil you like anything.

LEON. That's okay, Dad.

GREGOR. And then people would like me, wouldn't they?

LEON. They do now. Look at their faces. They're smiling at you. Even up there. (*He points to the audience.* GREGOR *looks out, pleased.*)

GREGOR. (*To the audience.*) Yes! I see! Oh, God bless you. You don't know what this means to me.

LEON. Then, let us go and sign the adoption papers and notify Sophia's family. Are you ready, Dad?

GREGOR. Let my just watch them smiling at me again. (*To the audience.*) Thank you. Thank you all of you. Maybe we can all have lunch together next week . . . In the meantime, you're all invited to my son's wedding! (*To* LEON, *as they exit.*) The first thing I'm going to do is have your shoes bronzed!

(*They are gone. Wedding decorations fly in as we hear bright, cheerful music.* SNETSKY, SLOVITCH, MISHKIN *and* YENCHNA *are dancing. All dressed in their best.* GREGOR *and* LENYA *approach from opposite sides of the stage. The music has slowed down to a processional.*)

SCENE 2

MISHKIN. Doesn't Mrs. Zubritsky look beautiful?

YENCHNA. Isn't it bad luck for the mother of the bride to see the postman before the wedding?

(*He hides behind* YENCHNA.)

SNETSKY. This is it, Slovitch—after two hundred years the curse will finally be gone.

SLOVITCH. I just had a terrible thought.

SNETSKY. What's that?

SLOVITCH. Suppose they lift the curse and I find out I was really dumb in the first place?

LENYA. They're coming! They're coming! Quiet, everyone! I have a sponge cake in the oven.

(LEON *appears.*)

LEON. (*To the audience.*) Remember, if I still appear stupid, I'm only pretending. It's all part of the plan.

LENYA. (*To* GREGOR.) You must be very proud of him.

GREGOR. He's been my son for ten minutes and he's never given me a moment of trouble.

(*The* DOCTOR *and* SOPHIA, *in bridial gown, appear.*)

YENCHNA. There but for me goes her.

MISHKIN. I hope she remembers to give me her change of address.

(*The* MAGISTRATE *appears.*)

MAGISTRATE. We are gathered here today, dear friends, to witness the joining of two souls in holy matrimony. It is only the good will and generous benevolence of our dear friend the Count that makes this blessed union possible.

ALL. Thank you, Count.

MAGISTRATE. Will the groom step before me.

GREGOR. That's you, *mein kind*.

(LEON *steps forward.*)

MAGISTRATE. And will the bride step forward.

(SOPHIA *steps out, but* LENYA *restrains her.*)

LENYA. No, Sophia, the bride! The bride!

DOCTOR. (*To* LENYA.) What's the matter with you? (*He places* SOPHIA *next to* LEON.)

SOPHIA. Leon, your plan was brilliant.

LEON. Thank you, Sophia.

MAGISTRATE. And who giveth away this bride?

DOCTOR. I giveth away this bride.

MAGISTRATE. Why do you giveth away this bride?

DOCTOR. Because he asketh me for her. And I nod-deth my head. And he taketh her.

MAGISTRATE. Do you, Leon, son of Count Gregor Mikhailovitch Breznofsky Fyodor Yousekevitch —

ALL. (*Shaking.*) Tremble, tremble, tremble, tremble . . .

GREGOR. No, no. Not today! You don't have to do it today. It's a holiday.

ALL. Oh, thank you . . . Very kind . . . How nice of you . . .

MAGISTRATE. Do you, Leon, take Sophia, to have and to hold from this day on?

LEON. I have.

MAGISTRATE. No. I do.

LEON. You do?

MAGISTRATE. No, *you* do.

DOCTOR. He will. He does, Say it.

LEON. "He will, he does." I said it.

DOCTOR. Don't say what I say. Say what he says.

LEON. What did he say?

GREGOR. "I do." Just say "I do"!

LEON. My papa says I do!

GREGOR. I'm beginning to hate this curse, I swear to God.

MAGISTRATE. And do you, Sophia, take Leon, in sickness and in health, for better or for worse, for as long as you both shall live?

SOPHIA. I do.

LENYA. With a brain like that she could have gotten anyone.

MAGISTRATE. The ring, please.

GREGOR. I have it. The ring that Casimir

Yousekevitch was going to place on the young Sophia two hundred years ago. (*He gives* LEON *a huge ring.*)

LENYA. What an onion!

MAGISTRATE. Place the ring on her finger.

(LEON *has great difficulty getting it on her finger.*)

LENYA. He's not going to be very handy around the house.

MAGISTRATE. Repeat after me, please: "With this ring, I thee wed."

ALL. With this ring, I thee wed.

MAGISTRATE. Just the bride and the groom, thank you.

LEON AND SOPHIA. With this ring, I thee wed.

MAGISTRATE. Before I pronounce this holy union, is there any among you who has just cause or reason why Leon and Sophia should not be joined in eternal wedlock? (*Pause.*) Then with the power invested in me as Chief Magistrate of the village of Kulyenchikov, I now pronounce thee—

GREGOR. (*Stepping forward.*) Welllll, maybe there's one tiny little thing.

MAGISTRATE. You have an objection to this marriage?

GREGOR. You bet I have! This boy is not my son . . . This son is not my boy!

LEON. What are you saying, Father?

GREGOR. You think I'm crazy? Why should I give up a cute little bundle of noodle brains like her?

LEON. But the adoption papers . . .

GREGOR. They're false. You trusted me so much you didn't even read them. Here are the documents as proof. I did not adopt him, I divorced him! According to these documents, we are not father and son, we are no longer husband and wife!

LENYA. Dear God, my daughter almost married a divorced woman. (*She faints in the* DOCTOR'S *arms.*)

SOPHIA. Leon . . . Is this part of the plan?

LEON. No, Sophia. I'm sorry.

GREGOR. But fear not, dear friends. I may be a venomously treacherous snake, but I'm not a wet blanket. There will be a wedding.

DOCTOR. My daughter will not marry an impostor.

GREGOR. An impostor, no. But a Yousekevitch, yes! You have pledged your daughter's hand in marriage, good doctor, to a Yousekevitch. And a pledge once given must be honored.

MAGISTRATE. That is the law. I helped write it myself.

DOCTOR. It's true. I even voted for it.

GREGOR. And I am the only true Yousekevitch here.

SOPHIA. Leon, will you not object to this marriage?

LEON. What can I do, Sophia? I am helpless.

MAGISTRATE. Come on. Come on. I haven't all day.

GREGOR. Say the words. Let's get it over with. There's been a hotel room booked for this honeymoon for two hundred years.

DOCTOR. I'm sorry, daughter. With all my heart, truly sorry. (*He places* SOPHIA *next to* GREGOR.)

LENYA. At least she'll get better dinners at his place.

MAGISTRATE. Dearly beloved—

GREGOR. We did that part. We heard that. I do. Ask her, she's the one.

MAGISTRATE. And do you, Sophia, take Count Gregor, for as long as you both shall live.

LENYA. Say it, darling. You'll be rich and smart. It's better than happiness.

SOPHIA. Goodbye, Leon . . . goodbye forever. I do.

MAGISTRATE. Then with the power invested in me as chief magistrate of the village of Kulyenchikov—

LEON. You didn't say the other part.

MAGISTRATE. What other part?

LEON. The part if anybody objects, and I object.

GREGOR. What's that?

MAGISTRATE. On what grounds?

LEON. On the grounds that I didn't receive my urgent letter yet.

GREGOR. What kind of grounds is that?

MISHKIN. I have an urgent letter for schoolmaster Tolchinsky.

LEON. For me? Whatever could it be?

GREGOR. Finish the ceremony while he's reading the letter.

MAGISTRATE. I can't do that. It's against the law.

DOCTOR. It's true. I even voted for it.

(LEON *has taken letter from* MISHKIN. *He sits down to read it. All except* GREGOR *surround him and listen.*)

LEON. It's bad news, I'm afraid. My uncle and sole remaining relative has just died in St. Petersburg leaving me nothing but all his debts.

SNETSKY. When you're going downhill, it gets faster at the bottom.

LEON. Before he died, he said he blamed all his misfortunes on the selfish and vindictive character of his distant relatives and that even changing his name to Tolchinsky never helped him escape destiny's finger.

DOCTOR. What was his name before Tolchinsky?

LEON. Yousekevitch.

YENCHNA. Oh-oh!

GREGOR. Those distant relatives will haunt you every time!

SOPHIA. Leon! Do you realize what this means?

LEON. No. What?

DOCTOR. He'll know in a few minutes. Schoolmaster, take your place next to my daughter. This time she's going to marry the right one!

LEON. (*To the audience.*) It didn't say that at all. It's a bill from my former college saying I still owe them for last year's tuition.

SNETSKY. Hurry, Leon, hurry.

LEON. (*To the audience.*) I have planted the bomb in their minds. I now pray God—for the explosion! (*He rushes to* SOPHIA'S *side.*)

MAGISTRATE. Hurry up. Places, everyone. I don't want to spend the rest of my life marrying this girl . . . Are we ready, everyone!

ALL. Ready!

MAGISTRATE. Do you, Leon—

LEON. I do.

MAGISTRATE. And do you, Sophia—

SOPHIA. I do.

MAGISTRATE. If there is anyone here who objects—

ALL. No one objects!

MAGISTRATE. Going once . . . Going twice . . . Going three times . . . That's it! I now pronounce you *man and wife*!

(*There is a loud thunder clap. The stage darkens, then gets lighter. All have fallen to the ground except* LEON, *who watches them.*)

SNETSKY. I have never heard a noise like that in all my life.

SLOVITCH. It felt as though my head had cracked open.

SNETSKY. Like What?

SLOVITCH. Like my—head had cracked open. (*He and* SNETSKY *look at each other.*) I'm afraid to ask it.

SNETSKY. Go ahead. Ask it.

SLOVITCH. But what if we're wrong?

SNETSKY. And what if we're right? . . . Ask it! . . . *Ask it!*

SLOVITCH. Cat?

SNETSKY. Cat. C-a-t, cat!

SLOVITCH. Dog!

SNETSKY. Dog. D-o-g, dog!

SLOVITCH. Oh, my God, it's a miracle!

SNETSKY. Miracle. M-i-r-a-c-l-e, miracle!

MISHKIN. Yenchna! . . . Yenchna—seven and five?

YENCHNA. Twelve.

MISHKIN. And twelve?

YENCHNA. Twenty-four.

MISHKIN. And forty-eight?

YENCHNA. Seventy-two! . . . Name five world capitals.

MISHKIN. Athens, Bucharest, Cairo, London, and—(*He is stuck.*)

LEON. You can do it!

MISHKIN. Constantinople!

(*They all cheer.*)

MAGISTRATE. (*Rises.*) The quality of mercy is not strained; it droppeth like the gentle rains from heaven.

(SLOVITCH *and* SNETSKY *are up.*)

SLOVITCH. That's beautiful. Did you make that up?

MAGISTRATE. I think so. Where else would it have come from?

LENYA. Nikolai! I—I feel funny. Weak in the knees.

A dizziness in my head.

(*The* DOCTOR *helps her up.*)

DOCTOR. It's all right, my dear. Your blood is just pulsating from the excitement. Sometimes that can cause the adrenal glands to oversecrete, resulting in a sudden rush to the head.

LENYA. I—I never knew you were such a brilliant doctor.

DOCTOR. I'm just an average doctor. I worry about you bacause—I love you, my dear.

LENYA. And I love you, Nikolai. Even when I couldn't say it, in my heart I knew I loved you.

SOPHIA. Leon . . . Are you now as you were before I became what I am?

LEON. I am more than I have ever been or dreamed could be possible.

SOPHIA. I love you, Leon.

LEON. I adore you, Sophia.

GREGOR. You mean it's over? The curse is over?

DOCTOR. See for yourself, Count Gregor.

YENCHNA. Land! I should have put my money in land. You can never go wrong with real estate.

(SNETSKY *and* SLOVITCH *leave.*)

MISHKIN. It depends, of course, on the political situation. With a czarist government, land reform is a very delicate issue.

(YENCHNA *and* MISHKIN *leave.*)

GREGOR. Such brilliant conversation. All my power over them is gone.

DOCTOR. Power is a useless weapon over the enlightened, Count Gregor. We are all equal citizens here.

LENYA. You mean men are all equal citizens. Women have been subjugated long before there were any curses.

DOCTOR. Lenya, you know I love you, but that's a very radical point of view. (*The* DOCTOR *and* LENYA *leave.*)

SOPHIA. It was your faith and courage that won over ignorance.

LEON. No, it was your pure heart and trusting soul that gave me that faith and courage. It was love that destroyed the curse, Sophia, not my puny efforts.

SOPHIA. I don't wish to argue the point, Leon. I just think you should allow me room to express my own views.

LEON. I welcome your views, Sophia, but I think you should have all the facts before you become so adamant.

(SOPHIA *leaves.*)

GREGOR. Well, you got your wish, schoolmaster.

LEON. Yes . . . What about you, Count Yousekevitch? What are your plans now that you're intelligent?

GREGOR. Thanks to you, I'll probably have to work for a living now. Well, cousin, my congratulations. I wish you a long and happy marriage.

LEON. Thank you . . . any may I wish the same good fortune to you.

GREGOR. Please. I've been cursed once in my life, I know when I'm well off. (*He leaves.*)

LEON. (*To the audience. During his speech, the cast*

members appear as he mentions them.) When you think of it, it's not such a bizarre story, after all. Be honest. Haven't you all met someone in your life who came from a place like Kulyenchikov? An aunt, an uncle, a neighbor . . . your boss! Of course, once the curse was lifted, we became like any other small town or village in any other part of the world, susceptible to all the "ups and downs" of normal life — well, the magistrate, for example. (*The* MAGISTRATE *appears.*) After two more years in office, greed got the better part of him and he was convicted for taking bribes for political favors. He served two years in jail and eventually sold his memoirs for a fortune. (MISHKIN *appears.*) Mishkin gave up the postal service and became a writer. He wrote a six-hundred-page story about the Curse of Kulyenchikov and sent it off to a publisher. Unfortunately, it got lost in the mail. (YENCHNA *appears.*) Yenchna, a shrewd business woman, put all her money in real estate and now owns seventeen houses in Kulyenchikov, including Count Gregor's. And as an investment for the future, she bought land in six other towns that had curses on them. (SLOVITCH *appears.*) Slovitch, with all his life savings, bought four more butcher shops in a village that really needed only one and went bankrupt in a month, confirming his greatest fears that with or without a curse, he didn't have much brains. (SNETSKY *appears, walks like a dandy*) Snetsky, with his newly acquired intelligence, found his sheep, gathered his wool, and became a wealthy philanthropist. (GREGOR *appears in a monk's robe.*) Count Yousekevitch became more and more lovable, studied theology, and is now the local monk. During the drought seasons he goes up on the hill and prays to God to throw water down on us. (LENYA *appears, looking officious.*) My dear mother-in-law,

Mrs. Zubritsky, suddenly found a voice of her own. She became the first woman mayor of Kulyenchikov and eventually consul governor of the Northern Ukraine Sector. Her husband sees her by appointment only. (*The* DOCTOR *appears.*) Dr. Zubritsky became one of the finest doctors in all of Russia. He became the personal physician to the royal family and was recently elected to the Academy of Sciences. However, he still has trouble opening jars. (SOPHIA *appears, carrying a baby.*) As for Sophia, she was—and still is—a miracle. Not that we don't have our differences, not that all our days are blissfully happy, but she has a wisdom that can never be found in books. She has, in turn, become my teacher, and I have learned there is no spirit on earth, evil or otherwise, that can destroy a pure heart of devoted love. As for myself, I remained a schoolmaster and dedicated my life to the education of the unenlightened . . . After all, there are so many Kulyenchikovs in this world.

CURTAIN

FURNITURE AND PROPERTY PLOT

Furniture plot
Zubritsky house: two chairs, table, swivel chair
Built in: desk, armoire, cabinet

ACT I—Preset
S.R.
Leon's satchel w/ map, clipping, cardboard
Handkerchief
Pocket watch
Small book pack
Ram's horn
Shepherd's rod
Coins
Broom (or preset inside butcher's shop.)
Chicken (plump?)
Bucket & towel
Monocle
String bag

Onstage
Doctor's desk:
   papers
   pens
   prescription pad
Samovar—S.R. of armoire
Curse book (on cabinet w/ dust)

S.L.
Mailpouch w/ postcard & mail
Flower basket w/ newspaper & flowers (one white)
Stethoscope (or on doctor's desk)
Coins

String bag
Whistle

ACT II—Preset
S.R.
Chicken to pluck
Bucket
Ram's horn
Shepherd's rod
Mail pouch w/ urgent letter
Large book pack (5) including math book
Pocketwatch
Small apple
Pocket knife
Whistle
Shopping bag (or inside butcher shop)
Ring in box
Legal papers
Broom
Lunch bag
Baby
Small book pack

O.S.
Newspaper (butcher shop door)

S.L.
Cow
Whistle
Brass candle holders w/ candles (2)
Matches
Monocle
Newspaper?
String bag
Prayer book (and pencil)

COSTUME PLOT

LEON
Brown Suit — aged
Sweater vest — grey
Shirt with Collar put on
Tie
Cap
Ankle boots
Tee Shirt
Underwear
Socks
Tights (allergic to wool)
Wedding —
   Embroidered wedding shirt
   Braided leather thong-belt
   Sash
Jewelry — watch in vest

SNETSKY
Russian Trousers
Shirt of two layer nets
Suspenders (unseen)
Stockings in leg wrappings
Shoes — woven
Backpack
Tee Shirt
Underwear
Socks
Brown Hat
Wedding —
   Red tie
   Broom with flowers
Coda —
   Sheepskin vest
   Designer Ram's horn case

MISHKIN
Britches
Uniform jacket — Act II and Coda
Vest
Shirt
Boots
Cap
Underwear
Tee shirt
Socks
Wedding —
   Embroidery shirt
   Sash
   Flowers on Mail Bag
Coda — Jacket

SLOVITCH
Britches
Apron
Embroidered Shirt
Boots
Straw Boater
Tee Shirts
Underwear
Socks
Wedding —
   Bow Tie
   Flowers on Hat
Coda — Remove flowers

SOPHIA
ACT I —
Lime green net blouse on green underbodice
Hair ribbons — blue

Blue (aqua) skirt
Aqua Kid shoes
Stockings
Undergarments
Change — nightgown and slippers

ACT II —
Blue Organza blouse
Blue silk strip skirt
White organza apron (pinafore)
Wedding —
   Wedding Dress
   Head piece with veil
   Satin Boots
   Coin necklace
   Gold braid in Hair
Coda — Replace Act II dress without pinafore add shawl

COUNT GREGOR
Riding Britches
Embroidered Vests
Baldrick
Shirts
Overcoat
Cap
Cravat
Tiepin
Watchchains
Boots
Wedding —
   remove cape
   add coat
   baldrick
   embroidered vest

Coda—
   remove everything but pants vest and shirt
   Benedictine Monk robe with Rope belt

YENCHNA
Head wrap
Dress (jumper)
Blouse
Apron
Petticoat
Stockings—colored
Shoes—half boots
Undergarments
Wedding—
   Flowered Hat
   Wedding overblouse
   Gold slippers
Coda—
   Hat
   Glasses
   Muff

MAGISTRATE
Underwear top
Shirt and Vest
Trousers
Overcoat with sash
Grey gloves
Top Hat
Tee Shirt
Underwear
Boots
Socks

Wedding—
  Add flower to hat
  Magistrate's medallion

LENYA
ACT I—
Dress with flowered skirt
Stockings
Shoes—taupe kid
Undergarments
Wedding—
  Wedding dress
  Headpiece
  Coin necklace
  Gloves—white
  Purse
Coda—
  Hat
  Pendant watch on chain
  Medals pinned to original dress
  Remove wedding hat and dress

DR. ZUBRITSKY
Trousers
Vest
Shirt
Bow Tie
Spats
Lab coat
Shoes
Underwear
Tee Shirt
Socks

Arm garters — mismatched
Wedding —
   Frock coat
   Bought shirts with embroidered collar and cuffs
   Flower on Lapel
Coda —
   Remove frock coat
   Add lab coat